BRAIDS &BOWS

FOR KIDS

Publications International, Ltd.

Louis Weber, C.E.O.
Publications International, Ltd.
7373 North Cicero Avenue
Lincolnwood, Illinois 60646

Manufactured in USA

8 7 6 5 4 3 2 1

ISBN 0-7853-0075-9

Contributing writers: Janis Bullis and Mary Beth Janssen-Fleischman

Janis Bullis is a crafts designer, writer, and educator who has worked for numerous crafts and fashion magazines, fabric manufacturers, and retailers. She is a member of the Society of Craft Designers, Hobby Industries of America, and Fashion Group International, and holds a B.A. in Home Economics Education.

Mary Beth Janssen-Fleischman is a hair designer, crafter, and International Artistic Director for Pivot Point Beauty School. She also serves as Artistic Director for *Design Forum,* a major trade publication for the hair salon industry.

Photos by Siede/Preis Photography

Illustrations by Craig Rex Perry

Royal Model Management models: Melynda Fraundorfer; Joy Kunishige; Ann Svane

Stewart Talent Management models: Tenisha Davis; Courtney Kelly; Jennifer Zalud; Lauren McCauley; Jessica Vilchis

Pictured on front cover, left to right: Ribbon Headband; Gathered Rosette with Basic Braid; Ponytail Wheel

Contents

Introduction

Hair ornaments come in a variety of sizes, styles, and shapes, in a range of colors and textures, and in endless combinations of ribbons, fabrics, beads, and baubles. For every mood, for every occasion, for every whim, you'll find ornaments that *you* can create. Feminine, sporty, glamorous, daring, elegant, wild, subdued, exciting—you can make them yourself or with a friend. Even better, make them *for* a friend, or your daughter or granddaughter.

Perhaps you'd like to try a new hairstyle. Or maybe you have a daughter or grandchild who wants a special look for a party—try an intricate herringbone design or classic side rolls. Or she might prefer a bun or a basic braid. From a simple pullthrough ponytail to a patterned French braid, you'll learn techniques that you can use in dozens of ways. Best of all, you can use the techniques and ideas you find here to develop fantastic new designs on your own. Mix hairstyles and bows, mix designs and fasteners, mix materials and methods, or use the information you find here as a starting point to come up with original creations.

GETTING STARTED

Before you begin, take some time to look through the book and get an idea of what kinds of projects you can try. Look at the headbands, combs, barrettes, and hairstyles to find something that catches your eye. Look at the techniques and materials to find something you're comfortable with.

Before you decide to create one of the hair ornaments, look the entire project over. Make sure you'll be content with the finished product. Make sure you feel confident about performing each step. Make sure that the materials and equipment are available and affordable.

After you've selected a project, make a list of all the materials you'll need to complete it. Give some thought to the color, style, and pattern of the ribbon or fabric and of any beads, appliqués, or other components. Make a list of everything you'll need to shop for. You may be overwhelmed by the variety of materials you have to choose from at the store. The list will help keep you on track, but don't be afraid to cut loose and enjoy yourself. You might get some new ideas to try on your project, or you might see some things that you want to use for your next effort.

Back at home, set up an area where you have room to work. You'll be measuring, cutting, sewing, ironing, and so on; be sure you have enough space to set up your materials and do your work comfortably. A large desk or table will do nicely, but you'll want to cover it with newspapers or oilcloth to protect the surface. Before you get started, set up your equipment and materials in an orderly fashion to help keep the work and fuss to a minimum.

You say you're really anxious to get started? You don't want to wait until you've had a chance to go shopping? No problem. Start off with one of the hairstyles! All you need for that is a good brush, coated hair bands, and maybe a hairpin or two.

KNOW YOUR MATERIALS

If you're new to this type of craft making, you should take the time to learn a few basic things about the things you'll be working with. Virtually all of the materials used in this book can be found at any local craft or fabric store. You might also try looking at specialty stores or novelty and costume shops.

Barrettes come in several lengths and sizes from small to extra long. The spring clip type of barrette is preferable because of its holding power and durability. You may find these barrettes easier to work with if you remove the spring clip before you begin the project; if you're going to be tying or wrapping things around the barrette, removing the clip is essential.

Hair combs are available in a wide variety of widths and colors. Spacing between the teeth of the comb also varies; the finer your hair is, the closer the teeth should be spaced. Most craft and fabric stores carry combs that are clear or neutral in color. Colored combs may be found in the hair accessory section of a local variety store.

The range of ribbons is tremendous—colors, patterns, materials, textures, widths. The projects in this book require ribbons from 1/8" to 2 1/2" wide. The best ribbons for bow making include woven-edged satin and ribbed grosgrain ribbons. These two types are softer and more workable than the somewhat stiffer craft varieties. Wired ribbons are another interesting option. The outer edges have wire running through them, making them more rigid and allowing you to mold the final shape to enhance the fullness of the design. Narrow ribbons are used primarily for stringing beads or holding charms or other ornaments. Grosgrain ribbon provides the best surface for painting.

Beads, trinkets, and appliqués come in an almost endless variety.

Make your selections based on mood, wardrobe, or whim. Be daring and creative in your choices.

A number of projects require craft wire, which you can find at your local craft store. A medium-weight wire is best; it's both sturdy and easy to work with.

TOOLS OF THE TRADE

Most of the bow making projects require some sort of equipment. In each of the projects that do, you will find one or more of the following symbols indicating the equipment you'll need for that project.

Wire cutters are needed for those projects involving craft wire. Needle-nose wire cutters are convenient for manipulating the wire. The grasping ends allow you to wrap and twist the wire tightly, maintaining tension but sparing your fingers.

You're sure to want quality scissors; your best bet is to invest in a good fabric-cutting pair available at the fabric or craft store. For our purposes, a medium or small pair is suitable; it'll do the job without being unwieldy. Pinking shears may be desirable for a zigzag effect along the edges of fabric or ribbon. Do not use these types of scissors to cut wire; this will dull the blades and perhaps even chip the cutting edge.

You will need a tape measure, ruler, or yardstick. Choose whichever device you are most comfortable working with. For most projects, you'll need to measure some materials to the proper length before beginning. In some instances, you may want to measure a bit long to have some extra material to work with; this is especially helpful when you're forming a long strip of ribbon into loops or bows. You may also find your ruler useful in measuring materials as you're working with them, to make sure you've left enough ribbon for the tail of a bow or to make sure a loop is the proper size, for example.

An iron will hold creases in your fabrics or ribbons, making them easier to work with and giving them a crisp, neat look. The iron is also effective for sealing plastic or vinyl material. When working with delicate materials such as satin, iron the material with a dampened towel or cloth over it. The iron will most often be used on a low or medium no-steam setting. Always follow the manufacturer's instructions for use, care, and safety when using an iron, and be sure to exercise caution.

Glue guns are a marvel for this kind of work. They take what can be a messy task and turn it into something quick, clean, and easy. A high-temperature gun is best for these types of projects. Always carefully follow manufacturer's instructions for use, care, and safety when using a glue gun. Exercise caution; the gun and the glue can reach temperatures of 350° F.

You will want a well-stocked sewing kit available to you so that you have an assortment of needles and thread. Embroidery needles and thick thread or monofilament line are good for securing heavy materials, but in most instances a regular needle and thread will suffice. Use thread colors that will blend with the ribbon that you're working on. A thimble may be a welcome item, especially when working on thicker materials.

Some projects also require straight pins or safety pins. The straight pins are used primarily for holding large pieces of fabric or ribbon together as you're stitching them. The safety pins are helpful for feeding elastic through hemmed material.

You may find it helpful to use a seam sealant, available at your local craft or fabric store. Apply a small amount to the cut edges of ribbon and fabric to keep them from fraying. Clear nail polish, used sparingly, serves the same purpose.

WHAT ABOUT HAIR?

The incredible ornaments you will find in this book are only part of the story. You're also going to learn to create a variety of hairstyles, and the techniques you learn can be adapted to styles that you create for yourself or someone special.

Some of these styles are quick and simple. You can do them any time, anywhere without a lot of fuss. A few are more complicated. They may take a little time and effort to execute, and they may take more than a little practice to master. Keep working at a technique until you're comfortable with it; all that's required is a bit of patience.

You may want to use styling products. Used properly, they can make it easier for you to work with the hair, and they can help you achieve a neater finished look. They can also help to keep the style in place. Depending on the hair, these products may not be necessary. A light misting with water might be enough, or you could even work with the hair dry.

Pomade will remove static, control flyaway ends, and give a glossy shine to the hair. It is meant to be used in small amounts, however. Apply some to one hand and rub your palms together to liquefy it. Then run your hands lightly and evenly through the hair.

Gel will also help to control the hair, but it gives you a wetter look than pomade does. You can work gel into the hair before you begin to style it, or you can use it to smooth down loose or stray hairs after you've finished.

Hair spray will hold the finished design in place. You can also apply it in spot areas as you work if the hair is somewhat unmanageable. Alcohol-free hair spray is probably better for your hair, but it provides less holding power.

pinwheel

Fresh and fun with a hint of glamour, the pinwheel bow radiates from the center to create a circular pattern. Polka dots and smoochy red lips make it memorable.

WHAT YOU'LL NEED

1⅓ yards ribbon, ⅞″ wide
three novelty lips
2¾″ barrette

1 Cut the ribbon into eight 6″ pieces. Trim the edges of each piece at an angle as shown.

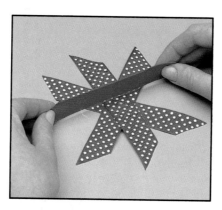

2 Place a drop of glue on the center of one piece of ribbon and glue another piece of ribbon across it. Glue each of the remaining six pieces on to form a circle.

3 Glue the lips to the center of the pinwheel.

Simple yet fancy, this pinwheel uses a slightly different technique. The ribbons are twisted once at the center before being glued together. This works best with thin, delicate material such as satin.

Glitzy, bright, lavish—this design is for those occasions when something extra special is called for. Brightly colored feathers are glued on top of a ribbon pinwheel and accented by a burst of curly ribbons.

4 Glue the pinwheel to the top of the barrette.

ponytail puff

Wispy, fine, and delicate, these gathered strips of netting create a feeling of elegance and classical beauty. They add sophistication to a simple braid. For an extra touch, tie another piece of netting to the bottom of the braid.

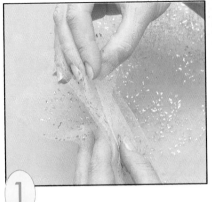

① Neatly lay the four pieces of netting on top of each other. Make sure the edges are aligned.

② Sew a row of running stitches lengthwise through the center of the pieces of netting.

③ Pull the thread ends to gather the netting up tightly. Tie thread ends into several knots to secure. Trim excess thread.

④ Sew the coated hair band securely to the center of the gathered netting.

⑤ Separate the layers of netting and fluff them up.

Gluing large sequins to the netting before you begin will give a whole different feel to the finished piece. The work may be a bit tedious, but the result is very cool.

A quick and neat way to add some color is with heavy thread. Just sew embroidery thread into the netting in long, loose stitches before you begin.

Basic Braid

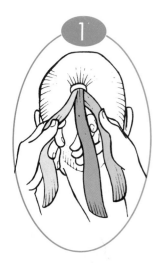

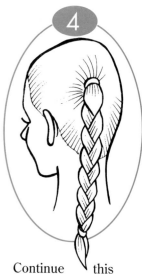

Fasten a ponytail at the crown of the head with a coated band. Divide it into three equal strands. Hold the left strand in your left hand. Hold the other two strands in your right hand exactly as shown; with your palm facing up, the right strand is between your thumb and forefinger and the center strand is between your forefinger and middle finger.

Turn your right hand over so your palm is facing downward. This will make the right strand cross over the left strand so that they switch positions.

Now hold the right strand in your right hand. Hold the other two strands in your left hand; with your palm facing up, the left strand is between your thumb and forefinger and the center strand is between your forefinger and middle finger. Turn your left hand over so your palm is facing downward. This will make the left strand cross over the center strand so that they switch positions.

Continue this procedure, alternating from right to left until the whole ponytail is braided. Fasten the end with a coated band.

shoelace bow

This one's as easy as tying your shoes, and the effect can be smashing when you combine materials to make it more intricate. Adding them on these side braids brings a new twist to an old hairstyle.

WHAT YOU'LL NEED

18" strung sequins

three 18" ribbons, 1/8" wide

1 1/2" barrette

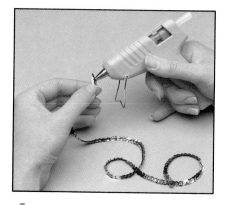

1 If you have to cut the strung sequins to the proper length, put glue on the ends of the string to keep the sequins on.

2 Hold the sequins and ribbons together about 4 1/2" from the ends. Form a loop about 2 1/2" long.

TIP

You can put these bows on barrettes, combs, or ponytail holders or you can tie them directly onto the end of a braid or the base of a ponytail.

3 Wrap the materials loosely around the base of the loop to form a small circle around it and then feed the materials through the circle to form a second loop, just as if you were tying a shoelace.

4 Pull the two loops in opposite directions to secure the bow, just as if you were tying a shoelace. Adjust the loops and the tails so the two sides are symmetrical.

5 Glue the barrette to the back of the bow.

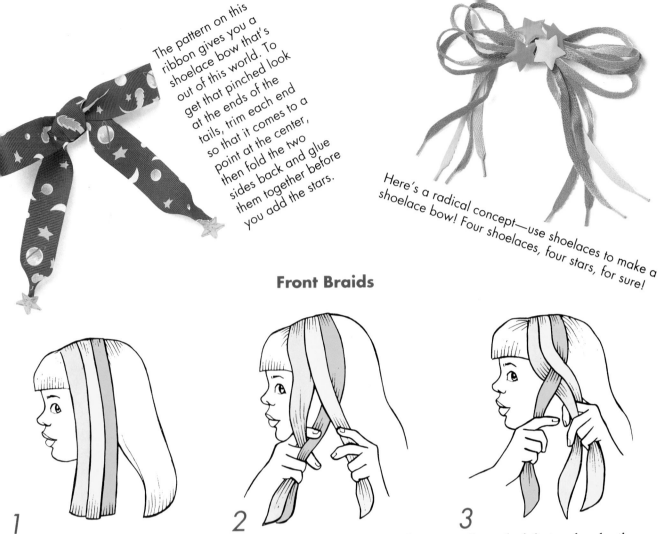

The pattern on this ribbon gives you a shoelace bow that's out of this world. To get that pinched look at the ends of the tails, trim each end so that it comes to a point at the center, then fold the two sides back and glue them together before you add the stars.

Here's a radical concept—use shoelaces to make a shoelace bow! Four shoelaces, four stars, for sure!

Front Braids

1
Create a center part. Working on one side of the head, gather the hair between the front hairline and the ear. Divide the hair into three equal strands.

2
Cross the right strand under the center strand and pull the center strand to the right. This will make the two strands exchange positions.

3
Cross the left strand under the strand that is now in the center and pull the center strand to the left. This will make these two strands exchange position.

4
Continue crossing the strands in this way until the entire section of hair is braided. Secure the braid at the end.

5
Repeat this procedure on the other side of the head to create a second braid.

looped barrette

Colorful ribbons and novelties combine to create large, loopy barrettes for all occasions. Make one just for the artist in you, or select your own clever novelty to glue between loops. Any way you do it, it'll be a masterpiece!

WHAT YOU'LL NEED

3¾" barrette
craft wire
1⅓ yards ribbon, 1½" wide
6 crayons

1 Open barrette and remove spring by pulling at center. Set spring aside. Slip craft wire through hole in end of barrette and twist to secure. Wrap wire around barrette several times.

2 Pinch ribbon approximately 3″ from end. Place on barrette at wired end and wrap wire around ribbon and barrette several times to secure.

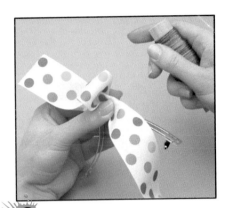

3 Pull up about 3″ of ribbon and make a loop about 1½″ tall. Pinch ribbon and wrap wire around ribbon and barrette several times to secure.

4 Continue making loops and securing them to barrette with wire. You should be able to make approximately 12 loops and still have enough to leave a 3″ tail of ribbon at end of barrette.

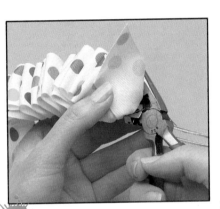

5 Slip wire through hole at end of barrette and twist to secure. Trim wire end. Trim ribbon ends evenly and at a 45 degree angle. Replace spring in barrette.

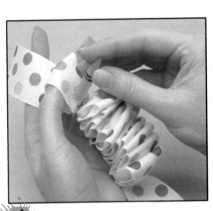

6 Cut crayons in half and glue cut end to barrette at random between loops of ribbon.

For this you'll need two pieces of rick rack, each 1⅓ yards long. Run them up and down and glue securely between the loops.

For holiday sleigh rides, this variation uses bells glued to the end of gathered ribbon.

staCKed bow

This bow provides just the right accent to your Western wear. The red bandanna stands out sharply against dark hair; if you're a blonde or a redhead, you might want to try a different color—maybe light blue.

WHAT YOU'LL NEED

bandanna
craft wire
10″ leather strip
1½″ concha
two wooden beads
four plated beads
2¾″ barrette

Cut two strips of material from the bandanna, one 12″ × 3½″ and the other 9″ × 3½″.

2 Glue together the ends of each strip of material to form them into two loops.

3 Pinch together the center of each loop to form a bow. Wrap craft wire around the center of each bow to secure it.

4 Place the small bow on top of the large bow and wire them together at the center. Fluff out the loops of the bows as needed.

5 Fold the leather strip in half. Insert the looped center through one of the holes on the concha and back through the other hole. Put the loose ends of the strip through the loop and pull to tighten.

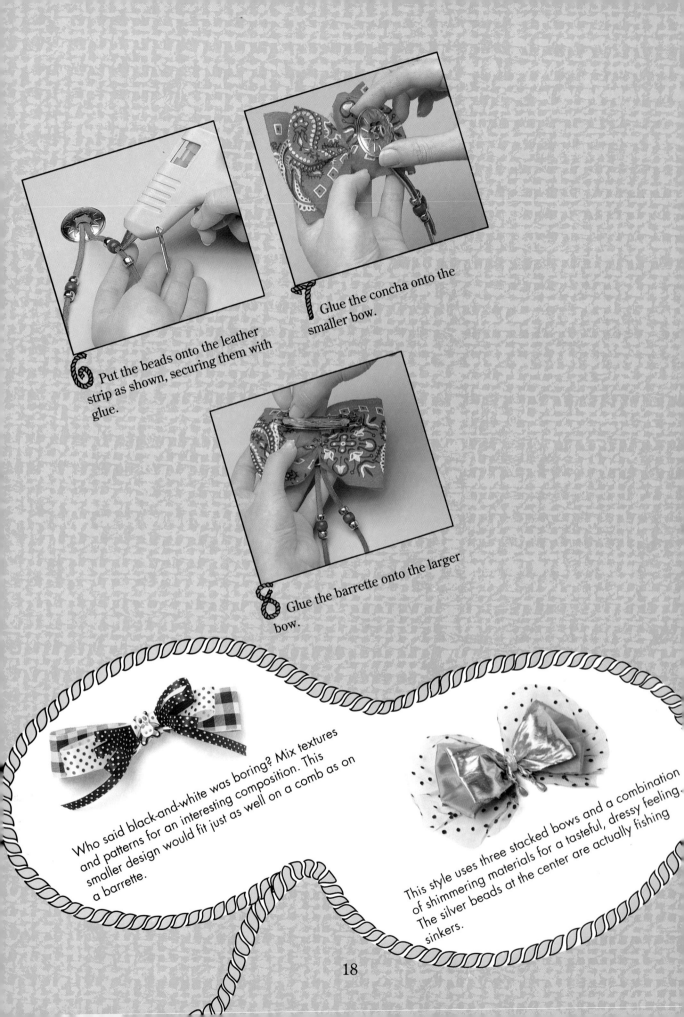

6 Put the beads onto the leather strip as shown, securing them with glue.

Glue the concha onto the smaller bow.

8 Glue the barrette onto the larger bow.

Who said black-and-white was boring? Mix textures and patterns for an interesting composition. This smaller design would fit just as well on a comb as on a barrette.

This style uses three stacked bows and a combination of shimmering materials for a tasteful, dressy feeling. The silver beads at the center are actually fishing sinkers.

Four-Strand Round Braids

Gather up the hair on one side of the head from the front hairline to the ear. Divide it into four equal strands. Cross the inside left strand over the inside right strand as shown.

With your right hand, reach behind the two inside strands and grasp the outside left strand. Bring the outside left strand behind the two inside strands . . .

. . . and back over the inside right strand. In essence, this makes the outside left strand and the inside left strand switch places.

With your left hand, reach behind the two inside strands and grasp the outside right strand. Bring the outside right strand behind the two inside strands and back over the inside left strand. In essence, this makes the outside right strand and the inside right strand switch places.

Continue braiding in this way, bringing the outside strand behind the two inside strands and then back over one of them, until the braid is long enough to reach the crown. Fasten the braid at the crown with hairpins.

Repeat this procedure on the other side of the head. Secure the two braids together at the crown.

Divide the hair that's left over from the braided sections into four strands. Braid this hair using the same technique. Secure the braid with a coated band.

ribbon headband

Bright polka dots and a touch of shiny purple make this headband POP! It's a nice touch any day you're looking to have some fun. These headbands work well with any kind of hair—short, long, thick, thin, whatever.

WHAT YOU'LL NEED

plastic headband
lightweight quilt batting, 2" × 17"
2½ yards ribbon, ⅞" wide

½ yard scroll braid, ½" wide
1 yard ribbon, 1½" wide
6" plated beads

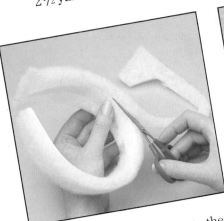

1 Glue the quilt batting to the outside of the headband. Trim batting even with edge of headband.

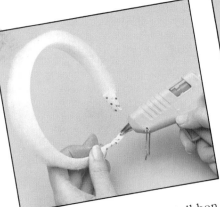

2 Cut a 2" length of ⅞" ribbon. Wrap and glue 1" of ribbon around one end of the headband. Glue and fold remaining 1" of ribbon to the inside of the headband. Repeat on the other end.

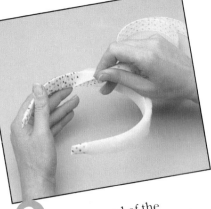

3 Cut one end of the remaining ⅞" ribbon on an angle and glue it to the inside of one end of the headband. Wrap the ribbon diagonally around the headband, overlapping ¼" each time.

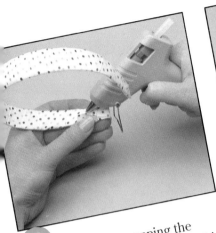

4 Continue wrapping the ribbon around the headband in this way. When you reach the other end, cut the ribbon on an angle and glue it on the inside of the headband.

5 Glue the ½" scroll braid to the inside of the headband. Set headband aside.

6 With right sides facing up, place the remaining ⅞" ribbon on the 1½" ribbon. Hold the ribbons together between your thumb and finger about 5" from one end to make a tail. Form the next 6" of ribbon into a loop and hold between your thumb and finger. Continue looping the ribbons as shown until you have two loops and one tail on each side.

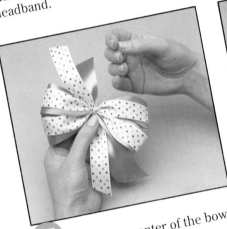

7 Pinch the center of the bow together and sew it securely.

8 Wrap and glue the plated beads around the center of the bow. Glue bow to top of headband.

Add a little something to a plain ribbon by sew buttons onto the headba after you've made it.

For a formal event in the spring or summer, you can have this lovely floral arrangement. Insert a grouping of silk flowers under the ribbon every other time you wrap it around the top of the headband.

beaded barrette

You've never seen anything like this before. This is art in motion, this is rattle and shine, this is bold and brassy, loud and jazzy, and it's sure to become one of the faves in your hair's wardrobe.

WHAT YOU'LL NEED

2¼″ safety pins, one gold and one silver
1⅜″ safety pins, five gold and five silver
1¼″ safety pins, 40 gold and 40 silver
spaghetti beads, 40 gold and 40 silver
2¾″ barrette

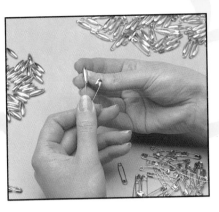

1 Put the 40 silver beads onto the 40 gold 1¼″ safety pins. Put the 40 gold beads onto the 40 silver 1¼″ safety pins.

If you use fewer beads, the safety pins will become more a part of the design. Create different patterns by changing the size, color, shape, or order of the beads. There's no limit to what you can do.

2 Put four of the beaded safety pins onto each of the 1⅜″ safety pins as shown. Alternate the color of the beaded pins—gold, silver, gold, silver.

Plastic beads will give you a flurry of color. This pair of barrettes would look great at the base of two pigtails or at the top of two braids.

3 Glue the 2¼″ safety pins to the barrette as shown. They should lie head-to-foot, and they should be angled outward a bit. Once you've set the safety pin on the barrette, put on more glue to secure it.

4 Attach the 1⅜″ safety pins to the 2¼″ safety pins as shown. Put the first one through the holes at the ends of the 2¼″ safety pins. Alternate the color and the direction of the 1⅜″ safety pins.

5 Continue attaching the 1⅜″ safety pins in this way across the barrette. Put the last one through the holes in the ends of the 2¼″ safety pins.

multiloop bow

Loops, loops, loops, and more loops! Use one basic technique to create this styled tangle of ribbon, or give yourself a classic look by making fewer, neatly formed loops. You could also add extra loops to make it even more outlandish!

WHAT YOU'LL NEED

1²/₃ yards ribbon, 1″ wide
craft wire
seven pieces of ribbon, ¹/₈″ wide and 5″ long
seven heart beads
2³/₄″ barrette

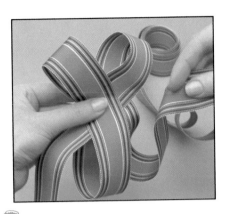

1 Hold the 1″ ribbon between your thumb and forefinger approximately 3″ from the end to leave a tail. Make a 3″ loop by bringing the ribbon to the left and then back under. Hold the loop securely between the thumb and forefinger. Bring the ribbon to the right and begin forming another 3″ loop.

2 Bring the ribbon back over to form a loop and hold it between the thumb and forefinger. Bring the ribbon to the left and then back under to form a third loop next to the first one.

3 Continue looping the ribbon right and left, over and under, until you have four 3″ loops on either side of your thumb and forefinger, for a total of eight loops. You should be left with a second tail about 8″ long. As you are looping, maintain tension on the center area and arrange the loops so they spread out neatly.

4 Wrap craft wire around the center of the bow to secure the loops; position the wire so there are four loops and a tail on either side. Twist the wire securely and trim any excess.

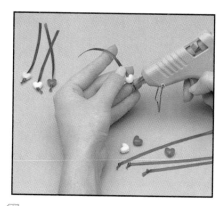

5 Using the long tail, make a small loop at the center as shown. Feed craft wire through the loop and wrap it around the center of the bow to secure the loop in place. Twist the wire securely and trim any excess. Trim the ends of the tails on an angle so that they are even.

6 Make a knot at the end of each piece of ⅛″ ribbon. Put a heart bead on each ribbon and glue it in place just above the knot.

7 Glue the ⅛″ ribbons together at the top ends. Put the top ends inside the center loop on the bow and glue them securely.

This bow was made with a thinner, longer ribbon. The loops are floppy and numerous, the colors are bright, and the clown makes the whole thing even more whimsical.

Legend has it that worry dolls like the ones on this bow can help to free you from your cares. This design uses a wide, wired ribbon and fewer loops for a more subtle effect.

8 Glue the barrette to the back of the bow.

Pullthrough

1 Pull back a section of hair from each side of the head and gather the sections together in a ponytail at the crown with a coated band. Reach down behind the gathered hair and grasp the ponytail as shown.

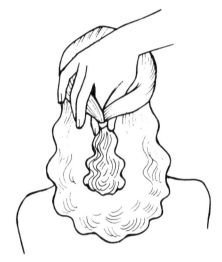

2 Pull the ponytail up through the gathered hair.

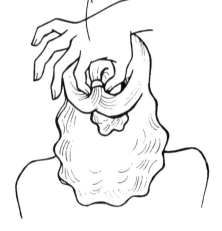

3 Flip the ponytail over and let it drop back down.

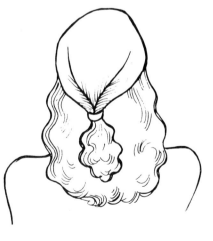

TIP

To make the design a bit more interesting, give each section of hair a twist or two before you join them together in the ponytail.

ponytail wheel

Wild, loose, and fun! Ponytail wheels feel great, and they're such attention getters. Every time you move your head you create a new splash of color. Slip the wheel onto a loose ponytail, or use it to liven up a chignon or bun.

NOTE
Use pinking shears to cut the pieces of fabric and give them a distinctive pattern on the edges.

WHAT YOU'LL NEED

16 pieces of fabric, 1″ wide and 10″ long, various colors
coated hair band

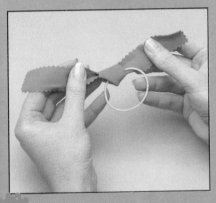

1 Tie one piece of fabric securely on the coated hair band.

2 Tie three more pieces of fabric on coated hair band, alternating colors to create a pattern.

3 Tie the remaining pieces of fabric to coated hair band following the same color pattern. There should be enough material to go halfway around the band.

For an even louder, wilder look, use curled ribbon in neon colors. You can buy curled ribbon, or soak regular ribbon in liquid starch and then wrap it tightly around a pencil until dry.

Color isn't the only way to get attention. This version uses texture, pattern, and shine to make it stand out.

Understated but still noticeable, this version alternates heavy cloth with painted netting. With the materials going all the way around the coated band, the wheel becomes much larger and fuller.

simple bow

Do up this simple yet classic bow in a nautical theme. The gold appliqué anchor is bound to the shimmery white satin ribbon by a gold-link chain. Cast off any hair design with this one.

WHAT YOU'LL NEED

1⅓ yards wired ribbon, 2½″ wide
craft wire
5″ wired ribbon, 1½″ wide
anchor appliqué
24″ plated chain
2¾″ barrette

1 Hold the 2¹/₂″ ribbon about 4″ from the end to leave a tail. Make a 4″ loop, bringing the ribbon under and holding it between your thumb and forefinger. Make another 4″ loop on the other side, bringing the ribbon over and holding it between your thumb and forefinger.

2 Make another 4″ loop next to the first one, again bringing the ribbon under and holding it between your thumb and forefinger.

3 Direct the ribbon to the other side of the tail, so that the tail is between the ribbon and the second loop.

4 Bring the ribbon over to make a fourth loop. Put the end of the ribbon under the top layer of ribbon in the center and bring it out between the first and third loops. You now have four loops with one tail between the first and third loops and one tail between the second and fourth loops. Trim any excess ribbon from the tail.

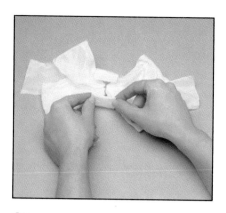

5 Wrap craft wire around the center of the bow to secure. Wrap the 1½″ ribbon around the center to cover the wire and glue the ends together.

6 Fold the chain in half, drape it at the center front of the bow as shown, and glue it in place. Glue the anchor on top of the chain.

7 Glue the barrette to the back of the bow. Trim the tail ends in a V-shape.

Express yourself with a basic white ribbon and lots of neon paints.

This vibrant burst of color is reminiscent of a Hawaiian lei. This bow uses narrow ribbon and silk flowers at the center.

A grouping of delicate roses floats atop swirling waves of pastel.

Three-Strand Ropes

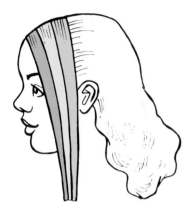

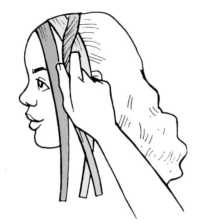

1 Gather up the hair on one side of the head from the front hairline to the ear. Divide it into three equal strands.

2 With your right hand palm down, grasp the right strand and turn your hand palm up so that you twist the strand; do this two or three times. Then cross the right strand over the center strand so they switch positions.

3 With your left hand palm up, grasp the left strand and turn your hand palm down so that you twist the strand; do this two or three times. Then bring the left strand under the center strand so that they switch positions.

4 Continue twisting and braiding the hair in this fashion, alternating from right to left, until you have a strand long enough to reach the nape of the neck. You'll have to maintain tension on the strands and handle them carefully to keep them twisted. Secure the strand at the nape of the neck with hairpins.

5 Repeat this procedure on the other side of the head. Secure the two strands together at the nape of the neck and let the rest of the hair hang down naturally.

gathered rosette

Rosettes are quick and easy to make, and you can do them in almost any size. Gather up your favorite ribbon or trim, then accessorize with flowers, buttons, or appliqués. Put a small rosette on a hook-and-loop fastener instead of on a barrette; it makes a perfect ornament for a baby sister or a favorite doll.

WHAT YOU'LL NEED

10″ ribbon, 1½″ wide
7″ ribbon, ⅞″ wide
2½″ metal barrette
heart button

3 Pull both thread tails of running stitches to gather ribbon and form a rosette. Tie thread tails into several knots to secure rosette. Trim excess thread.

2 Turn ribbon right side out, so the seam is inside the loop. Sew a row of running stitches along one long edge of ribbon beginning and ending at the seam. Do not cut thread tails.

1 With right sides together, match the ends of the 1½″ wide ribbon and sew a seam ¼″ from the edge to form a loop. Trim thread tails.

This large rosette was made with a silky, gilded material. The flashing holiday ornament at the center gives it a novel touch.

For a more elegant look, make rosettes with a fine white lace and top with a sil' flower.

4 Using the same technique, create a small rosette with the 7⁄8″ wide ribbon.

5 Glue large rosette to barrette, glue small rosette to large rosette, and glue heart button to small rosette. Allow to dry.

35

round-a-bow

Round-a-bows are a frilly, fluffy, lacy explosion! They're similar to scrunchies, but they don't have to be twisted to create an interesting style; this design stands on its own.

WHAT YOU'LL NEED

1 yard lace, 10″ wide

5″ elastic, ¼″ wide

Fold the lace in half lengthwise. At one end of the closed, folded side, sew a double stitch ½″ from the edge to secure the thread.

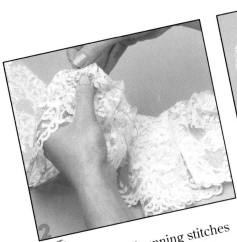

Sew a row of running stitches up the length of the lace on the closed, folded side, staying ½″ from the edge.

When you reach the other side of the lace, weave the needle through the lace to hold it in place. Attach a safety pin to the end of the elastic and feed it all the way through the seam you have just created.

Tie the ends of the elastic together in a double knot. Trim any excess elastic.

Remove the needle from the lace and gently pull on it to gather the lace around the elastic. Stitch the knotted ends of the elastic together securely. Trim any excess thread.

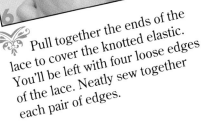

Pull together the ends of the lace to cover the knotted elastic. You'll be left with four loose edges of the lace. Neatly sew together each pair of edges.

Netting and satin create a soft, shimmery, exotic round-a-bow for a touch of mystery.

This round-a-bow was made from the leftovers of a pair of jeans that were cut into shorts. Cutting into the edges makes it loose and floppy and adds to the design by exposing the reverse side of the material.

Braided Chignon

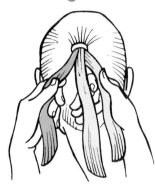

1

Fasten a pontytail at the crown of the head with a coated band. Divide it into three equal strands. Hold the left strand in your left hand. Hold the other two strands in your right hand exactly as shown; with your palm facing up, the right strand is between your thumb and forefinger and the center strand is between your forefinger and middle finger.

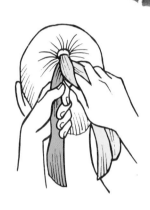

2

Turn your right hand over so your palm is facing downward. This will make the right strand cross over the left strand so that they switch positions.

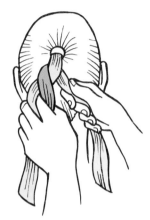

3

Now hold the right strand in your right hand. Hold the other two strands in your left hand; with your palm facing up, the left strand is between your thumb and forefinger and the center strand is between your forefinger and middle finger. Turn your left hand over so your palm is facing downward. This will make the left strand and the center strand switch positions.

4

Continue this procedure, alternating from right to left until the whole pontytail is braided. Fasten the end with a coated band.

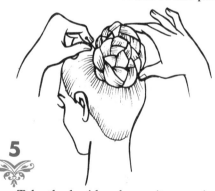

5

Take the braid and wrap it around its base at the crown to make the chignon. Use hairpins to secure the chignon to the hair near the scalp. Wrap the chignon in different ways to create new looks.

Simple and stylish, this bow is versatile and easy to make. You can top it with almost any type of novelty, and your choice of material will give you a bow that's understated or bold, elegant or expressive. Doll house shops are a terrific place to find some interesting novelties for the finishing touch.

gift box bow

WHAT YOU'LL NEED

three pieces of ribbon, 1½″ wide and 10″ long

metal barrette, 2¾″ long

novelty wrapped packages

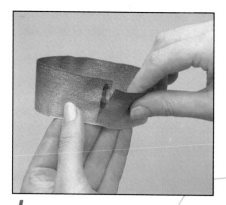

1 Overlap the ends of each piece of ribbon ½″ to form a loop. You may want to glue the ends together to make the loops easier to handle.

2 Pinch both sides of each loop together at the center to form a bow. Sew the pinched area of each bow to secure it.

3 Stack and glue the three bows together at the center in a pinwheel fashion.

4 Glue the barrette to the bottom bow.

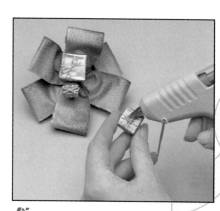

5 Glue novelties to the top of the bows.

NOTE

When gluing novelties to the bows, think about what direction the barrette is in. If you're putting on a picture or a message, make sure it will be right side up when the barrette is in your hair.

This bow brings a touch of spring with a few silk flowers and some chenille bumble bees. Silly but cute.

Add a personal touch with a photo of your pet, your best friend, some hunky guy, or even a picture you've drawn yourself. Just glue the picture to a piece of colored cardboard and slap it on the bow.

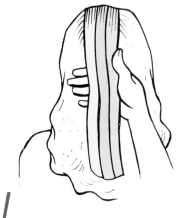

1
Comb all the hair back. Pick up a section of hair at the center front hairline and divide it into three equal strands.

2
Take the right strand and cross it over the center strand so that they switch positions. Take the left strand and cross it over the new center strand so that they switch positions.

3
Now comes the tricky part. Hold all three strands in your left hand exactly as shown. With your right hand, pick up a section of hair along the hairline to the right of the braid and add it to the right strand.

4
Take this right strand and cross it over the center strand so that they switch positions.

5
Now hold all three strands in the right hand as shown. With your left hand, pick up a section of hair along the hairline to the left of the braid and add it to the left strand.

6
Take this left strand and cross it over the center strand so that they switch positions.

NOTE
This is a difficult technique to master. Don't be discouraged if you have trouble the first time you try it. Or the second, third, fourth, or fifth time, for that matter. Keep at it; your fingers will eventually get the hang of it.

7
Continue in this way, alternating from right to left and adding new hair to each strand until all the hair has been picked up. Then continue braiding the three loose strands until all the hair is braided. Secure the braid with a coated band.

8
Now take the hanging end of the braid and fold it up and under to the nape of the neck. Secure it there with hairpins.

Easy to make and easy to wear, this headband works for sports, school, or everyday fun. Just slip it on and slip it off. It keeps your hair under control and adds a nice touch without much time or effort.

WHAT YOU'LL NEED

30″ satin ribbon, ⅞″ wide
30″ satin ribbon, ⅝″ wide
18″ elastic, ⅜″ wide

This style is great for infants who don't quite have a full head of hair. Use a few inches less material for a comfortable fit, and maybe add a cute appliqué.

1) Fold back each end of both ribbons ¼" to the wrong side. Iron the ends to form a sharp crease.

Add some contrast and texture to the headband by using a material that has eyelets in place of the satin ribbon. Simply run a colored ribbon back and forth through the eyelets before you begin. For a final touch, tie a bow with an extra piece of colored ribbon and sew it on.

2) With right sides up, lay ⅝" ribbon on top of ⅞" ribbon and center it from side to side. Pin the ribbons together to hold them in place. Neatly sew the two ribbons together along the edges of the ⅝" ribbon.

3) Attach a safety pin to the end of the elastic. Insert the safety pin between the ribbons at one end and use it to feed the elastic through the ribbons.

4) Remove safety pin. Overlap the ends of the elastic and sew them together securely.

5) Overlap the ends of the ribbon and sew them together securely.

plastic bow

This design offers you a window to display whatever special effects you can think of. The clear vinyl forms a "pocket" for your decorations to swim around in. In this version, the sequins will sparkle and shine with your every little movement.

WHAT YOU'LL NEED

clear vinyl, 6″ × 14″

netting, 16″ × 18″

sequins

craft wire

2³/₄″ barrette

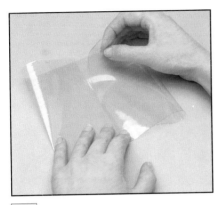

1 Fold both ends of the vinyl over to the middle and overlap them ½″.

2 Run a medium iron over the bottom ¼″ of the vinyl to seal it closed. Use only the edge of the iron and work slowly to be sure you get a straight, complete seal.

3 Cut a 2″ × 18″ strip off the netting and set the strip aside. Bunch up the remaining netting and put it inside the vinyl. Fan the netting out as needed. Pour the sequins into the vinyl and spread them around.

4 Run a medium iron over the top ¼″ of the vinyl to seal it closed.

5   Pinch the vinyl together at the center to form a bow.

6   Wrap craft wire around the center of the bow to secure it. Wrap the strip of netting around the center of the bow several times and tie it securely. Trim any excess netting.

7   Glue the barrette to the back of the bow.

Create your very own aquatic ecosystem, complete with multicolored fish, crystal "bubbles," and a few shells. This one-of-a-kind tropical seascape is definitely a conversation piece!

You're sure to scare up some compliments when you wear this ghoulish design. Be resourceful; the centerpiece on this bow came from a cake decorating kit.

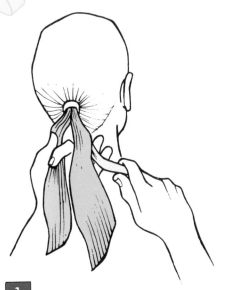

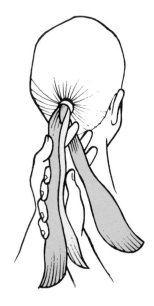

1

Fasten a ponytail at the nape of the neck with a coated band. Divide the ponytail into two equal sections and hold in the left hand as shown. Using your right hand, separate a small section of hair from the back of the right strand as shown.

2

Cross this section over to the left strand so that it becomes a part of the left strand. Run your right hand down the length of the left strand to smooth the hair together.

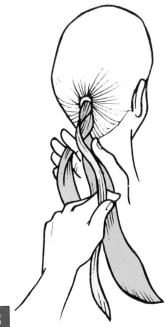

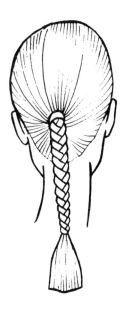

3

Move the two strands into your right hand and hold as shown. Using your left hand, separate a small section of hair from the back of the left strand and cross it over to the right strand so that it becomes a part of the right strand.

4

Alternating from the right strand to the left strand, continue separating small sections from the back of each strand and crossing them over to the other strand all the way down the ponytail. Secure the end with a coated band.

balloon barrette

This ornament is sure to be a crowd pleaser! The colors are a visual treat, and the balloons certainly create a festive mood. Perfect for parties or for when you're clowning around.

WHAT YOU'LL NEED

25 small balloons, various colors
2³/₄" barrette

1 Take four balloons of different colors and group them together, alternating their direction.

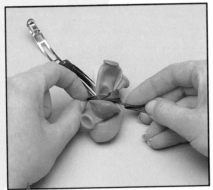

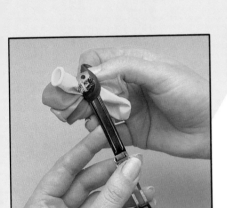

4 Continue adding groups of balloons along the length of the barrette in this way. Five groupings should be enough to cover the barrette. Adjust the balloons as needed for a balanced look. Replace the spring in the barrette.

3 Tie a knot in the fifth balloon to secure the group to the barrette.

Trick or Treat! Just for Halloween, begin by blowing up the balloons slightly and tying them on one at a time. Tie one black and one orange shoelace to the center and glue the bat to the knot in the laces.

2 Open the barrette clip and remove spring by pulling at center. Place the group of balloons on top of the barrette and wrap a fifth balloon around them at a slight angle.

Be my Valentine! Delicate red hearts and bright red balloons conjure up the sweetest images. For this variation, loop the ribbon along the length of the barrette and tie it down with the balloons.

Snap-On scrunchie

WHAT YOU'LL NEED

lightweight fabric, 8″ × 30″

6″ elastic, ¼″ wide

large snap, #3

heart appliqué

This unique idea turns one scrunchie into many scrunchies. Change the appliqué to match the day, your mood, or your outfit. Scrunchies look especially good in a ponytail up high on the head. Slip the ponytail through, twist the scrunchie, and slip the ponytail through again.

1 Fold fabric in half lengthwise so right sides are touching. Sew a seam ¼″ from the edge to form a tube.

You can accent this scrunchie with a different snap-on every day. Always attach the female half of the snap to the scrunchie and the male half to the button, novelty, or appliqué.

This variation will give you a different look for every holiday party you attend.

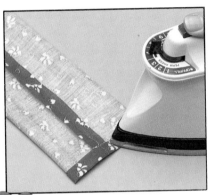

2 Fold sides of seam down and iron so they lie flat. At one end of tube, fold edge back approximately ½″ and iron so it lies flat to form a hem.

3 Turn tube right side out. Attach large safety pin to end of elastic and use it to help feed elastic through the tube.

4 Remove the safety pin. Overlap ends of elastic approximately ½″ and sew them together.

5 Insert unhemmed end of tube approximately ½″ into hemmed end of tube. Use a large pin to hold ends of tube in place and then sew them securely together.

6 Sew female half of snap to scrunchie, across from the seamed end. Sew male half of snap to heart appliqué.

classic bow

This timeless style is large and eye-catching but always in good taste. Wired ribbon works especially well with this design; it helps the bow to keep its shape.

WHAT YOU'LL NEED

27" wired ribbon, 2" wide
18" wired ribbon, 2" wide
craft wire
2¾" barrette

1 Begin working with the 27" ribbon. At one end, roll about 5" of the ribbon into a circle and hold it securely with the thumb and forefinger.

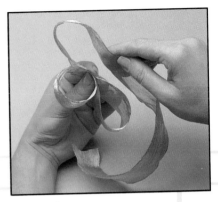

2 Using the next 5" of ribbon, form a 2½" loop to one side of the circle, again holding it securely in place between the thumb and forefinger. Make a second loop of the same size on the other side of the circle and again secure the ribbon between the thumb and forefinger.

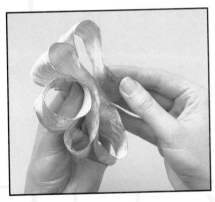

3 With the same method, make another pair of loops with the remaining ribbon; each loop should be about 3" long.

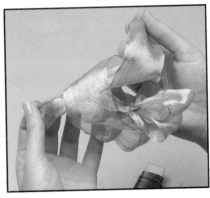

4 Feed craft wire through the circle and around to the back of the loops; secure the loops and the circle together with the wire. Feed the 18" ribbon halfway through the circle. Tie the ribbon in a tight knot in back of the loops, making sure the tails of the ribbon are the same length.

5 Trim the tails of the 18" ribbon in a V-shape. Glue the barrette to the back of the bottom loop.

NOTE

This is probably the toughest hairstyle in the book. Be sure you're comfortable making a basic French Braid (page 41) before you try to do this one.

French Underbraids

1

Begin by making an off-center part from the front hairline to the crown. Pick up a section of hair at the hairline on one side of the part and divide it into three equal strands.

Bring a little something extra to this design by gluing a novelty to the top of the bow. Pastel striped ribbon and a clown might make you think of the circus.

With a marker and a few wooden blocks from the craft store, you can turn this bow into a personalized gift for a friend.

5

Hold all three strands in the right hand as shown. With the left hand, pick up a new section of hair from along the part and add it to the left strand.

Festive red and gold ribbon and a small bell are suitable for a holiday, or any day for that matter.

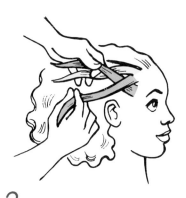

2
Cross the right strand under the center strand so that they change positions. Then cross the left strand under the center strand so that they change positions.

3
Hold all three strands in the left hand as shown. With the right hand, pick up a new section of hair from along the hairline and add it to the right strand.

4
Take the right strand and cross it under the center strand so that they change positions.

6
Take the left strand and cross it under the center strand so that they change positions.

7
Continue braiding in this way, adding new hair to the outside strand and then crossing it under the center strand, alternating from right to left, until you reach the crown. Secure the braid to the crown with hairpins.

8
Repeat this procedure on the other side of the head. Join the two braids together at the crown and secure them. Let the rest of the hair fall naturally down the back of the head.

barrette topper

Barrette toppers make a nice, broad platform for most anything you want to put on them—candy, painted squiggles, drawings, sequins, beads, charms, or just a fabric with an interesting pattern. Make yourself a pair of them and use them to pull your hair back to the sides.

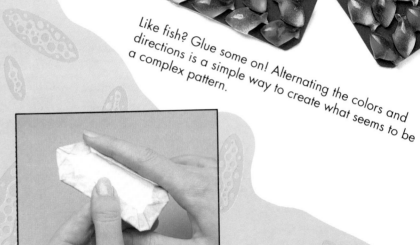

Like fish? Glue some on! Alternating the colors and directions is a simple way to create what seems to be a complex pattern.

1 Trim the corners of the fabric, batting, and cardboard to make them rounded.

2 Glue the batting on top of the cardboard.

3 Lay the cardboard and batting on top of the fabric, making sure they are centered; the cardboard and the wrong side of the fabric should be facing you. Apply a drop of glue to each corner of the cardboard and fold each corner of the fabric over so that they are glued together.

4 Apply glue to the four edges of the cardboard and fold the four edges of the fabric over so that they are glued together.

5 Glue the top of the barrette to center of the cardboard.

Plain white fabric, some acrylic neon paints, and a little creativity—that's all it takes!

57

ruffle ribbon

The ruffle ribbon is set off beautifully by a beaded pattern. The ribbon can stand on its own, but adding something can give it a formal look to coordinate with a special outfit.

WHAT YOU'LL NEED

1 yard ribbon, 2½″ wide
16″ craft wire
44 pearl beads
20 plated beads
2¾″ barrette

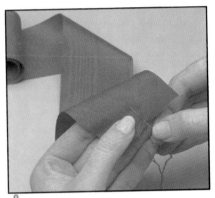

1 Secure the thread at one end of the ribbon in the center using a double stitch. The thread should be doubled and knotted at the end.

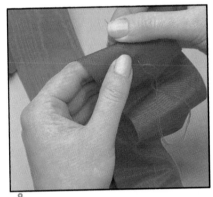

2 Neatly sew a running stitch down the center of the ribbon to the other end. The stitches should be approximately ½″ apart.

NOTE

The stitch size is an important part of getting the ribbon to gather properly. On thick ribbons, they should be ½″ apart; on thinner, more delicate material, they should be ¼″ apart.

TIP

Fold the ribbon in half before you sew to put a faint crease in it; follow the crease as you sew to keep the stitches in a straight line.

3 Hold the ribbon in one hand and the thread ends in the other. Carefully pull the thread in one direction and push the ribbon in the other to create the ruffle. When the ruffle is the desired length, tie or sew the thread ends securely in place. Trim any excess thread.

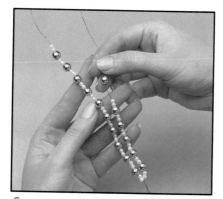

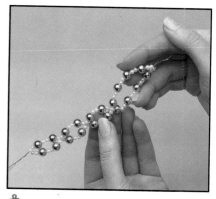

4 Bend the craft wire in half and twist the wire together a few times at the end with the bend.

5 Thread half the beads on one side of the wire and half the beads on the other side of the wire in an alternating pattern as shown—two pearl beads followed by one plated bead.

6 Twist the wire at every other group of pearl beads to create a pattern as shown. Do not twist the last group at either end of the wire.

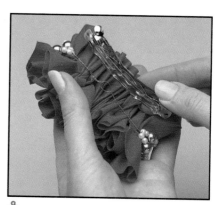

7 Place the beaded wire lengthwise across the top of the ruffle. Bring the ends of the wire around the back of the ruffle and twist them together securely. Trim any excess wire.

8 Glue the barrette to the back of the ruffle.

ke this kind of ruffle, use a
r ribbon and sew a narrow
tterned ribbon around the
dge of it before you start. Fold
he narrow ribbon back and
forth on itself as you sew for a
more intricate finish.

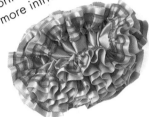

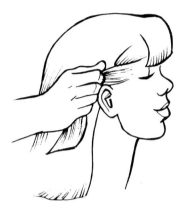

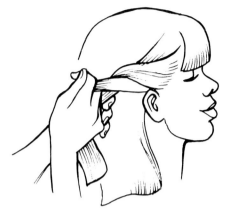

1

Pick up a section of hair from the hairline near the temple and hold it in your right hand palm up. Twist the hair by turning your hand palm down.

2

Transfer the twisted section of hair to your left hand and hold it securely. Pick up a new section of hair in your right hand as shown. Add this to the hair in your left hand and give the whole thing a twist.

netting makes for an airy,
spish ruffle, and the
himmering beads seem to be
floating above the material.
Handle the netting gently, and
use the glue sparingly when you
affix the beads.

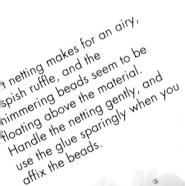

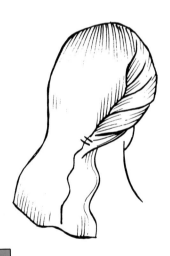

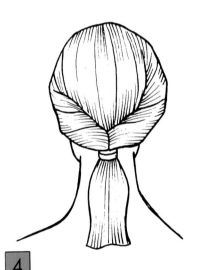

3

Continue back along the hairline, adding new sections of hair and twisting, until you reach the nape of the neck. Pin the hair securely with a hairpin.

4

Repeat this procedure on the other side of the head. Join the two twisted sections at the nape of the neck with a fastener and let the rest of the hair fall free.

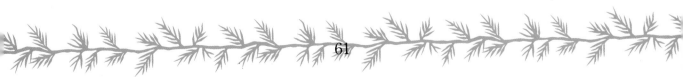

Wired Comb

Oh Great Pumpkin! This ornament can be as varied as your imagination. Here, Halloween theme wire is strung with black satin ribbon to add extra dimension and contrast to the design.

1 Wrap craft wire around the top of the comb between the first two teeth and twist it securely.

2 Place the novelty wire and ribbon along the top of the comb so that approximately 2″ of wire and ribbon extends past the end of the comb. Wrap the craft wire around the novelty wire, ribbon, and comb between the first two teeth of the comb.

3 Form a loop approximately 2″ tall with the novelty wire and ribbon. Use the craft wire to secure the loop to the top of the comb by wrapping it between the next two teeth of the comb.

4 Continue making loops and securing them with craft wire between the teeth of the comb until you reach the other side of the comb. Keep the size of the loops consistent.

5 Wrap the craft wire around the top of the comb a few extra times. Twist craft wire securely and trim off any excess. Trim the novelty wire and ribbon, leaving approximately 2″ extending beyond the edge of the comb.

Twisted Bun

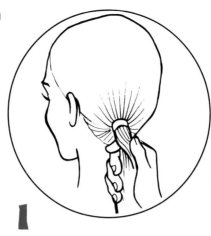

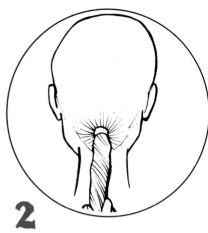

1 Make a ponytail at the nape of the neck with a coated band. Grab the ponytail just below the band and twist to the right.

2 Moving down the ponytail, continue twisting the hair to the right, maintaining an even tension, until the entire ponytail is twisted.

Set off fireworks when you wear this design! The shimmer and glimmer of these red stars are enhanced by the white and blue satin ribbons.

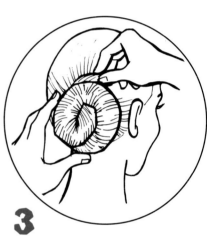

3 Coil the twisted hair in a circle around the base of the ponytail.

This comb has a group of long-legged flamingos high-stepping through colorful looped lacing. These loops are a bit smaller so the glued-on flamingos don't get lost.

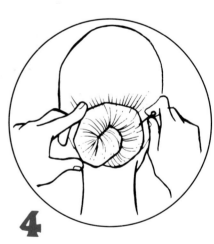

4 Using hairpins, secure the bun to the hair near the scalp.